I'm Thinking of a Dinosaur

Bela Davis

Abdo Kids Junior
is an Imprint of Abdo Kids
abdobooks.com

Abdo
I'M THINKING
OF AN ANIMAL
Kids

abdobooks.com

Published by Abdo Kids, a division of ABDO, P.O. Box 398166, Minneapolis, Minnesota 55439.

Printed in the United States of America, North Mankato, Minnesota.

052024

092024

THIS BOOK CONTAINS RECYCLED MATERIALS

Photo Credits: Getty Images, Shutterstock

Production Contributors: Teddy Borth, Jennie Forsberg, Grace Hansen

Design Contributors: Candice Keimig, Pakou Moua

Library of Congress Control Number: 2023948538

Publisher's Cataloging-in-Publication Data

Names: Davis, Bela, author.

Title: I'm thinking of a dinosaur / by Bela Davis

Description: Minneapolis, Minnesota : Abdo Kids, 2025 | Series: I'm thinking of an animal | Includes online resources and index.

Identifiers: ISBN 9798384900535 (lib. bdg.) | ISBN 9798384901235 (ebook) | ISBN 9798384901587 (Read-to-me eBook)

Subjects: LCSH: Dinosaurs--Juvenile literature. | Questions and answers--Juvenile literature. | Riddles--Juvenile literature. | Animals--Juvenile literature. | Zoology--Juvenile literature.

Classification: DDC 568.19--dc23

Table of Contents

Guess the Animal!

I'm thinking of a dinosaur.

Can you guess what it is?

I'm thinking of a dinosaur that lived on land.

clues

- lived on land

But it is not a Velociraptor!

I'm thinking of a dinosaur that lived in North America.

clues

- lived on land
- North American

But it is not a T. rex!

I'm thinking of a dinosaur that was medium sized.

clues

- lived on land
- North American
- medium sized

But it is not a Ceratosaurus!

I'm thinking of a dinosaur that ate plants.

clues

- lived on land
- North American
- medium sized
- ate plants

But it is not a Parasaurolophus!

I'm thinking of a dinosaur that walked on four legs.

clues

- lived on land
- North American
- medium sized
- ate plants
- walked on four legs

But it is not a Triceratops!

I'm thinking of a dinosaur that had **armored plates**.

clues

- lived on land
- North American
- medium sized
- ate plants
- walked on four legs
- had armored plates

But it is not a Stegosaurus!

Do you know what dinosaur I'm thinking of?

clues

- lived on land
- North American
- medium sized
- ate plants
- walked on four legs
- had armored plates

I'm thinking of an Ankylosaurus! Now it's your turn! What dinosaur are you thinking of?

Comparing Animals

	T. rex	Ceratosaurus	Triceratops	Ankylosaurus
lived on land	✓	✓	✓	✓
medium sized		✓	✓	✓
ate plants			✓	✓
armor plated				✓

Glossary

armored
wearing or being covered by armor.

plates
large, thick, bony pieces on the bodies of some dinosaurs, such as Stegosaurus, that may have helped protect them or control their body temperature.

Index